Harkening unto Jesus

HOPE AND ENCOURAGEMENT FOR YOUNG CHRISTIAN WOMEN

by Mary F. Caltenco

EABooks Publishing
Your Partner In Publishing

Cover design by Krystine Kercher
Orchid cover photo by Madllen, 2013; used by permission
of DepositPhotos; Saint-Petersburg, Russian Federation

Unless otherwise noted, scripture is taken from *The Holy
Bible, English Standard Version*. Copyright © 2000; 2001 by
Crossway Bibles, a division of Good News Publishers.
Used by permission. All rights reserved.

Scripture taken from the New King James Version®.
Copyright © 1982 by Thomas Nelson. Used by permission.
All rights reserved.

*Harkening Unto Jesus, Hope and Encouragement
for Young Christian Women*
By Mary F. Caltenco

ISBN: 978-1-952369-50-6

Published by EA Books Publishing a division of
Living Parables of Central Florida, Inc. a 501c3
EABooksPublishing.com

Dedication

To my beloved husband, Elias, who went to be with the Lord while I was writing this book. Your emotional support of my writing meant the world to me. I love you. I miss you. And I look forward to the day when I will see you again.

To God—all the glory.

Let the one who hears say,
"Come." And let the one who is thirsty come;
let the one who desires take
the water of life without price.

(Revelation 22:17)

Harkening

Our Lord calls us—let us hear,
There's a whisper of His tone.
We can all dismiss our fears
And find that we are not alone

For every longing in your heart,
His rivers of bounty flow.
With guidance, wisdom, and goodwill
To expel our human woe.

Come unto God—He's waiting;
He has summoned you by name.
Take the bliss His love imparts
You will never be the same.

Contents

Introduction

MANY YEARS AGO, MY husband and I visited Rome. While we were there, we visited the church of St. Peter. I'll never forget looking at a tall, white column inside with the words of Peter from John 6:68 inscribed on it: "Lord, to whom shall we go? You have the words of eternal life."

There has never been a time in history in which so many forces have converged to threaten the family. But the words of Peter continue to run through my mind: "Lord, to whom (else) shall we go?" He's the only one who possesses eternal truth, and He said we are here to be a light to the world (Matthew 5:14–16). In our day and time, He's calling us to step into the fullness of spiritual womanhood and shine brightly.

In an article by Mary Cagney in the April 6, 1998 issue of *Christianity Today*, Christian author and speaker Esther Burroughs is quoted as saying, "You older women of Christ, there is a generation of women out there longing to walk beside you . . .

Mentoring is not about cloning, but about helping women become like Jesus." With that in mind, my heart as a Christian woman is to pass on to younger Christian women what I've learned in my many years in walking with Jesus.

My own journey to a deeper faith began in the 1990s as a mother who was stumbling through everything in my pathway. My husband began to study the Bible and I took notice. Shortly thereafter, he suggested that I do it too. Around that same time, my friend Debbie Colon asked me to consider Bible Study Fellowship classes. As I immersed myself in the Scriptures, they gave me God's truth and hope, and God got bigger in my eyes. Those classes taught me what it means to develop an intentional spiritual life—a life not formed by an unyielding preoccupation with doing things my own way but that called me to harken (listen) to God's voice.

The older I get, the more I realize that harkening to the voice of God is the most important work we can do. We have many distractions in this world. If we really want to hear God, we must listen with soft-heartedness. God's goodness occurs every day, but we need to turn our eyes to Him to see it (Isaiah 49:15, Hebrews 1:3).

We must be open to listening to His Word and accepting it in our hearts. In doing so, we receive the blessings that strengthen us to fulfill its commands and teachings. Jesus emphasized the importance of our relationship with Him when He said He is the vine and we are the branches (John 15:5). He abides in us and we are to abide in Him. As this occurs, we are more and more attuned to what He has to say to us.

I've included ten bits of wisdom in this short book that I'd like to share with you. In each one, you'll find hope and encouragement to live in the fullness and luxuriant life of our Lord Jesus Christ as you seek to live for His glory.

This isn't meant to be a comprehensive list of everything you need to know as a young Christian woman who is chasing the heart of Jesus. It's just a few of the things I'm most passionate about. Take some time with me now to pull away and go on this journey with me as I point you to the Savior.

Your Purpose

*I cry out to God Most High, to God
who fulfills his purpose for me.*

(Psalm 57:2)

NOT LONG AGO, I encountered a period of adversity with dry eyes. One medical treatment after another backfired. As the months rolled by, I continued to pray for relief.

On a Friday evening, feeling a little heavy-hearted, I turned on TV and tuned in to the Christian Television Network (CTN). The Good Life had just begun. The founder of the program introduced himself as Bob D'Andrea. Jane, his wife, was also present. He mentioned his guest speaker would be Mr. Bob Armstrong, and they spoke briefly to open the program before transitioning to a time of music.

"Let's welcome Mr. Creed Warren," Mr. D'Andrea said. "He is going to bless us with his piano chords and song right now." His lyrics were so piercing and soothing that it jarred me out of my heaviness. I felt God speaking to me right there. His love and joy were palpable. Jesus assures us that not a hair falls from our heads without Him knowing about it (Luke 12:22–31, 21:18, Psalm 46).

After the song, Mr. Armstrong began to share his stirring story about his one-on-one personal compassionate encounter with Oral Roberts when Mr. Armstrong was a young man. Mr. Armstrong's parents had set high standards for him growing up, but he'd rebelled, and Mr. Roberts had challenged him, sending Mr. Armstrong's mind in search of God's truth.

Mr. Armstrong continued. "A new door swung open for me, and in time, I became ordained. Now, I'm the founder of Love-Link Ministries which, for decades, has taught leadership principles to 48,000 pastors and leaders in fifteen countries."

Next, Mr. Warren began to sing again, and there was a telephone number displayed on the TV screen to call when the song ended. I dialed the number, hoping to leave a message, however, to my amazement, a woman answered.

"This is Kim."

"Hello, Kim. I've been watching *The Good Life* and enjoying it. Can you please give me the name of the initial hymn that Mr. Creed Warren sang? It is so beautiful, but I missed the title."

"How nice to hear from you," she said. "I noticed your last name on the receiver. Are you related to Dr. Caltenco?"

"I'm his wife."

"I work with your husband. I'm Kim Armstrong. My husband is on the program today. I don't know the name of the song; however, I will most gladly give the message to my husband and you can expect his call Saturday."

"I'm so sorry for the interruption," I muttered. "Let's continue watching your husband on the program."

As the program progressed, Mr. Armstrong spoke about what the Lord was leading him to do. "For the past three years, I have ministered within five miles of ISIS-held territory in Kurdistan. My organization is called Operation Freed from ISIS, which helps to rescue girls and families directly from ISIS and rehabilitates them in safe houses in Kurdistan. This is just another organization and ministry God has blessed me with."

At the close of the show, Mr. D'Andrea turned over the microphone to Mr. Armstrong for his remaining words. "Are you hurting right now? God wants to use you right where you are. It doesn't matter who you are or what you do—you are important to God."

After the show, in faith, I settled into my writing couch with my blue notebook and attempted to write another Christian poem but struggled with my eyes. After several more attempts, my efforts felt futile, so I prayed. "Lord, what is Your plan for me now? I don't understand, but I trust You."

As time went by, I persisted in prayer. Then, one day, an answer came in the form of a small inner voice that I believed was from the Lord. He assured me that He would provide the vision I needed to accomplish a task for Him. "You can write a book about your stories and include your poems alongside them," the Lord said.

I could just feel it. My model was Philippians 3:13–14: "Brothers, I do not consider that I have made it my own. But one thing I do: forgetting what lies behind and straining forward to what lies ahead, I press on toward the goal for the prize of the upward call of God in Christ Jesus."

God holds us in the palms of His hands. His strong arms reminded me of His nearness (Psalm 89:13). In my insufficiency, His power was perfected in my weakness (2 Corinthians 12:9). His power is greater than me, allowing me to perform "good works, which God prepared beforehand," that I should walk in them (Ephesians 2:10), and He showed me what I could accomplish each day with Him (Isaiah 30:18–21, 2 Corinthians 9:8).

I didn't know what the particulars would look like, but I knew God would enable me to do the work to which He'd called me.

Within the week, a parcel came in the mail from Mr. Armstrong containing the name of the hymn I requested, as well as his book, *Razor's Edge*. It foretold of Mr. Armstrong's turmoil of being placed unjustly in federal prison for over a year. Years prior, he'd signed certain papers for a corporation, following the orders of the CEO, causing him to be implicated in a crime. He agreed to a plea agreement, even though he was absolutely innocent, because he could not raise $150,000 to defend himself.

When he was set free, he was determined to further the purpose of his ministry. He hoped to rebuild suffering, war-torn countries, both spiritually and materially. I couldn't help but admire his courageousness after coming out of such a horrific ordeal, and I admired the way he now lived so dangerously for the cause of Christ.

It is such a reminder not to quench the Spirit by cowering under the tyranny of "what ifs?" *What if I get hurt? What if it gets worse?* God is prompting us to invest our lives (Jeremiah 1:5) for the cause of Christ. He chose you and me. We are His mouth, hands, and feet to carry out His plan and work.

We were not created to live for ourselves. Instead, God created us to live for other people and for causes greater than ourselves. Jesus calls us to the servant way, so He set the example. He Himself said, "For even the Son of Man came not to be served but to serve, and to give his life as a ransom for many" (Mark 10:45). When we follow His example in servanthood, we join our Lord in His purposes.

Each of us has been given gifts, and as we exercise those gifts, we find purpose. What are your gifts? Do you sing in the choir, teach Sunday school, help with functions at the church or in children's ministry, or do you do something else—maybe even despite your weaknesses? I recall someone saying, "Take your sorrow and use it as fire to burn through the blockades standing in the way." I absolutely believe that.

You are young. Don't be overly concerned with choosing the wrong path as you serve God and people. Instead, talk to older trusted Christians in your life about ways you can serve and ultimately, find your purpose. Pray, asking for clear direction from God. Then be aware of the needs around you. As you do all three, God will show you what He wants you to do. And as you step into your purpose, you'll find great fulfillment.

Prayer of Purpose

Give me, O Lord, a heavenly vision
To make each day demand a count,
Inciting thy potential into action
Of vistas of what life is all about.

Father, teach me that I may teach
The priceless words though do disclose.
Consecrate thy words to rescue
The weary ones from all their foes.

Enlarge my burden for all the lost
Grieved at sin's enslaving power.
May my heart be possessed by thy love
Delivering them in their darkest hour.
Come Holy Spirit, quicken my prayer
Interceding for souls in their need
Give empowerment, health, and Your strength
Amid all their storms may peace exceed.

Spending Time
with God

Draw near to God,
and he will draw near to you.
Cleanse your hands, you sinners,
and purify your hearts,
you double-minded.

(James 4:8)

I FIRST MET MARY Ann Dunlap thirty-four
years ago after church. My husband, Dr. Caltenco,
introduced us. I learned that Mary Ann oversaw
the medical surgery floor at the hospital where
my husband worked. She worked with indigent
patients there. She was warm and engaging and
there was a certain tranquility of spirit that radi-
ated from her. I liked her right away.

Soon after, I noticed Mary Ann at church and made it a point to sit next to her. It wasn't long before we chatted about our children. She said she had three sons and a daughter. And I told her I had two sons who were in elementary school.

"Mary, why don't we pray for each other's children," she said one day. And it seemed to bond us as friends—a friendship that continues to this day.

Her dedication to the Lord always impressed me. She often stayed after church to pray.

As the years passed, our friendship grew, and one sunny summer day, sitting at her dining room table, I asked her about her devotional life.

"My prayer life has changed over the years," she said. "Years back, time was my most precious commodity. I was a nurse in the emergency room and a single mother with four children: a newborn, a one-year-old, a two-year-old, and a four-year-old.

"Being raised in church, I attended often. It really helped me to develop my prayer life. During our services, I always looked forward to the pastors' Bible readings and their explanations. Those little nuggets of truth of God's Word would guide me the whole day. At least most of the time. There were days when this wasn't the case. One of the children would fall and break a bone, or all four of my children would have the flu, or the hospital would call for 'all hands on deck.' But those trials changed me.

"My bedroom became the place I had my sacred time with the Lord before the children arose. I made a little sign out of popsicle sticks that read 'five minutes,' and I placed it on the bedroom door. They would see it and sit at the door and wait for me to come out. They were quiet because they knew how important it was to me. If I didn't have time with the Lord, I felt I was thrown into the day without being prepared.

"In the Gospel of Luke, God says, 'This is my beloved Son. Listen to Him.' It reminds me of when Mary sat at the feet of Jesus and listened to Him. God has a longing for us, and in response, we can have a longing for Him. Being still before the Lord put me in His presence."

While I was still sitting at Mary Ann's dining room table, I had another question for her. "When you were raising your children alone, what general counsels of Scripture guided you?"

"I was anemic, so 2 Corinthians 12:9 was important. It says, 'My grace is sufficient for you, for my power is made perfect in weakness.'" Then she named a few other Scriptures:

- The first one was Psalm 68:5–6: "Father of the fatherless and protector of widows is God in his holy habitation. God settles the

solitary in a home; he leads out the prison-
ers to prosperity, but the rebellious dwell
in a parched land."

- The second one was Matthew 28:20: "And
behold, I [Jesus] am with you always, to
the end of the age."
- The third one was Psalm 73:23–24:
"Nevertheless, I am continually with you;
you hold my right hand. You guide me
with your counsel, and afterward you will
receive me to glory."
- She pointed out that Joshua 1:8 reminds
us of how important it is to meditate. We
burn out when we try to do everything
ourselves.
- And she said that Psalm 46:10 encourages
us to let go, cease striving, and know that
He is God.

Hearing Mary Ann describe her time with God
in such a fashion reminded me of what George
Herbert, a seventeenth-century poet, wrote in
his poems, describing mankind's longing for God.
In his poem "The Pulley," one of my favorites,
he uses the pulley mechanism as a metaphor for
the restlessness of our hearts, which God uses to
draw us closer to Him. He says that when God created us, He bestowed wonderful gifts on us, such
as strength, beauty, wisdom, honor, and pleasure.

But God withheld the best gift, which is rest, so we would not find contentment or fulfillment in any of the other blessings, but only in God Himself. Because God still holds the gift of rest, we must turn to God to find it.

David passionately pursued God. In Psalm 27:4, he said, "One thing have I asked of the LORD, that will I seek after: that I may dwell in the house of the LORD all the days of my life, to gaze upon the beauty of the LORD and to inquire in his temple." He was desperate for God, and he brought every situation in his life to God. This was his first priority.

In Susie Larson's book *Your Sacred Yes: Trading Life-Draining Obligation for Freedom, Passion, and Joy*, she wrote, "We're not called to a busyness that drains us; we're called to an abundance that trains us."[1] And it all begins with having a foundation through the Word.

You can trust the Bible. It should be your final authority. Get to know how the Bible came into existence. Look at it as nuggets of truth in the form of a person, and that person is Jesus Christ (John 1:14). A doctor of divinity once told me that the anchor of your faith should be Christ's death and resurrection (Philippians 3:10), and to know that Christ is the only way to go. It's through the Word of God that the Spirit reveals us to God. The Bible was given to us to reveal God that we might know, love, and worship Him.

Talk to God about how you want to spend more time with Him and ask Him to help you evaluate or rearrange your day so you can do so. Talk to Him about not skipping prayer because you have a busy day. Talk to Him about your dreams, joys, sorrows, decisions, sins, and failures. Talk to him about your loved ones and all those you care about. And talk to Him about your love for Him, your appreciation for Him, and how you desire to be more like Him. Be honest with your feelings. Ask God to show you how to thrive. He has more in store for you than living in survival mode.

I recommend that you keep a time log, then evaluate it after a week. What can you do to spend more time with God? Less time on the phone with friends? Social media? TV? Maybe you need to trim some of your children's nonstop activities. This will give you more time to get into God's Word. His Word is His way of speaking to us today (John 1:1–5). Even if you have to schedule time on your calendar, do it.

In Charles Stanley's book *How to Listen to God*, he wrote, "We can be tired, weary, and emotionally distraught, but after spending time alone with God, we find that He injects into our bodies energy, power, and strength. God's spiritual dynamics are at work in our inner beings, refreshing and energizing our minds and spirits."[2]

In Thomas Merton's book *The Inner Experience: Notes on Contemplation*, he says to seek one thing alone—to purify your love of God more and more; to abandon yourself more and more perfectly to His will; and love Him more exclusively and more completely but also more simply and more peacefully with more total and uncompromising trust.

One way of spending time with God is to pause to think about Him, to contemplate who He is as you read Scripture. In the book of Ezekiel, the Lord traces the history of Jerusalem. It began with a foundling child who was unwashed and unwanted, but He didn't stop there. Ezekiel 16:8 says, "When I passed by you again and saw you, behold, you were at the age for love, and I spread the corner of my garment over you and covered your nakedness; I made my vow to you and entered into a covenant with you, declares the Lord GOD, and you became mine." Isn't that beautiful?

Here are eight practical steps you can take to spend time with God:

1. Start with five or ten minutes. You can expand the time as you go on. Early morning signifies a placement of prominence for the day when the mind is most refreshed, but it's not a one-size-fits-all. You'll always have something pressing to do—especially if you have young children. Make a

commitment to prioritize your time with God each morning.

2. Select a comfortable and quiet setting in your favorite chair or couch.
3. Make sure all devices and cell phones are off so you'll be free from distractions.
4. Clear your mind and think thoughts of gratitude toward God.
5. You may want to start with something from the New Testament, then transition to something from the Old Testament.
6. Whatever you are reading, pinpoint the verse that is meaningful to you and meditate on it.
7. You might want to end by reading the psalms of joy and lament. Reflect on how the psalmist spent time with God.
8. Think about what God is like in His attributes. Study them. Nothing has been of greater importance to growth in grace for me.

Union with Christ

In the wondrous time with Jesus

From flush of morn to cool of day

I am guided in varied stages

Through all the tangled maze

Oh, Jesus, how you love me
You never forget me at all
You open the door of mystery
And come to my aid when I fall

There were times I rushed past You
And stood on the field of defeat
Struggled and faltered on the way
You are here to make me complete

There is praise for time with You
A time to delight in Your love
A time set aside for hearing
With fullness of Your presence above

[1] Susie Larson, *Your Sacred Yes: Trading Life-Draining Obligation for Freedom, Passion, and Joy* (Minneapolis: Bethany House Publishers, 2015), 25.
[2] Charles Stanley, *How to Listen to God* (Nashville: Thomas Nelson Publishers, 2002), 100.

Recognizing Satan
and His Strategies

Be sober-minded; be watchful. Your adversary the devil prowls around like a roaring lion, seeking someone to devour. Resist him, firm in your faith, knowing that the same kinds of suffering are being experienced by your brotherhood throughout the world.

(1 Peter 5:8–9)

IN 2006, I ATTENDED the International Center for Biblical Counseling (ICBC), which is now called Deeper Walk International, in Indianapolis, Indiana, where I learned the basics of Christian counseling and developed the foundation for an understanding of a biblical worldview. I met Dr. Mark Bubeck who founded the ICBC there. He has since gone on to be with the Lord. I learned that while he was praying for revival awakening in 1967, he experienced a spiritual confrontation that thrust him into a study of spiritual warfare. That study led to him writing his first book, *The Adversary: The Christian Versus Demon Activity*, on the subject in 1975.

He brought me to full attention on this subject when he shared his testimony with our class that included a story about his daughter's direct battle with darkness. And it wasn't his family's last spiritual warfare. He said that the life of victory does not come with a quick fix and that it doesn't always lead to the enemy leaving right away. Instead, he stressed the importance of resisting him every day. To do so, he said, believers need a firm understanding of the kingdom of darkness and the strongholds that are under Satan's control.

He said the devil was and is a created being and that he is still fully answerable to God. He can only function within the prescribed limits set by his Creator (Job 1:6–2:7). And since he is a fallen angel, he oversees a kingdom of fallen angels that would seem to number as many as one-third of all the created angels (Revelation 12:3–9), which is an organized kingdom (Colossians 1:16, Ephesians 6:11–12).

The nineteenth-century French poet Charles Baudelaire wrote, "The devil's finest trick is to persuade you that he does not exist." In the providence of God, the devil has been quite successful in persuading his followers that he doesn't exist. Even popular culture trivializes Satan as one who sits on the shoulders of cartoon characters and comically whispers into their ears, twirling his pointed tail. Such depictions suggest that the devil is easily overcome. However, Matthew 4:1–11 tells us that there really is a Satan (Genesis 3:17) and that Jesus Himself was tempted (Luke 4:9–13).

In my life, Satan attacks when I'm ill, fatigued, discouraged, or in the decision-making process. He knows each of our weakest points and aims at them. What about you? What are your weakest points? Do you experience thoughts that cause you to wonder where they came from? Or maybe they cause you to wonder how or why you did or said something. There isn't one of us who hasn't experienced this at one time or another.

Accusations are Satan's favorite weapons against us. Revelation 12:9–10 (NKJV) explains it this way: "So the great dragon was cast out, that serpent of old, called the Devil and Satan, who deceives the whole world; he was cast to the earth, and his angels were cast out with him. Then I heard a loud voice saying in heaven, 'Now salvation, and strength, and the kingdom of our God, and the power of His Christ have come, for the accuser of our brethren, who accused them before our God day and night, has been cast down.'"

He is always present to accuse us. Have you heard his accusations? "You prayed and your prayers were not answered," he might whisper in your ear. "You are not one of the favored ones. You will never make it. You keep slipping up over and over again." Satan accuses us in hatred to make us dispose of or shun God's help. Satan even tried to accuse Joshua the high priest through his conscience as he stood before the angel of the Lord (Zechariah 3:1).

You can recognize how intimidating he is by his deceitful schemes. In Ephesians 6:11–12, Satan commands a demonic army. And then what does he do? He appears as an angel of light (2 Corinthians 11:14). Satan is pictured today as an evil-looking red creature with a tail, but in reality, he masquerades falsely, attempting to snare recent converts (1 Timothy 3:6–7). But he doesn't stop there.

Another one of Satan's schemes is to try to get you and me to justify a lack of forgiveness. Do you find yourself thinking, "Why should I forgive? This keeps happening over and over. Nothing is going to change." Have you heard him telling you this very thing? He wants to destroy us.

More so, Satan tempts you and me to be fearful (1 Peter 5:8–9). Do you realize that worry is a sin? I didn't. My closest friends in high school, Sophie Buttigieg and Carole Lobeck, nicknamed me "Worries" because I worried so often. The devil deceives us by placing thoughts in our minds that try to tell us that the current set of circumstances we are enduring is unusual. But this is a lie. Peter makes it known that you are not alone in your affliction. Many others go through it as well. Knowing that you are not alone, you can resist Satan by faith.

The evil one will also tempt you to excuse all fleshly sins (Ephesians 4:17–29). He wants to blind your spiritual vision. Paul names such things as lying, anger, stealing, corrupt speech, bitterness, and an unforgiving spirit in this passage. These are just some of the sins that will hurt us. Satan will try to get you to believe you can sin in secret, but don't fall for that. Sooner or later, your sin will be exposed.

There is only one way to overcome the wicked one, and that's having the Word of God abiding in you (1 John 2:14). That's how Jesus was able to defeat Satan in the wilderness. He quoted the Scriptures. We can defeat him by doing the same.

Spend some time in the Word this week looking up verses that will combat the specific schemes that Satan is using against you. Write the verses out by hand and carry them with you on an index card or in a notebook. Every time you feel like you are under attack, pull out the card or notebook and read the verse. As you do so, you are submitting yourself to God. This is the way to resist the devil.

James 4:6–8 says, "'God opposes the proud but gives grace to the humble.' Submit yourselves therefore to God. Resist the devil, and he will flee from you. Draw near to God, and he will draw near to you."

We've covered a lot of ground in this chapter. Let's do a quick summary of the ways that Satan attempts to deceive us: by prompting us to hold onto offenses, by attacking us when we are feeling tired or ill, by accusing us, by trying to get us to hold onto unforgiveness, by tempting us to fear, by attempting to get us to walk in darkness by covering our sins, and by tempting us to excuse our fleshly sins. Which of these schemes has Satan used to attack you?

Will you commit to combatting Satan by spending more time in the Word to tear down Satan's strongholds in your life? Understand that you are in a spiritual battle, so you must fight against Satan in the spiritual realm with the Word. 2 Corinthians 10:3–5 says, "For though we walk in the flesh, we are not waging war according to the flesh. For the weapons of our warfare are not of the flesh but have divine power to destroy strongholds. We destroy arguments and every lofty opinion raised against the knowledge of God, and take every thought captive to obey Christ."

The Shield of Faith

Take up the shield of faith
And rest in Christ Himself
Who absorbed the blows of temptation
And the demonic attacks He dwelt.

By trusting in God and His Word,
We lift up the shield of faith
And rest in Him as our protector
Not adding fuel to Satan's bait.

The Lord shields us from temptation
As we look upon Him daily
To help us walk in holiness
And walk His path faithfully.

The Lord does this all for His people;
He guards us that we might persevere
To prevail against the enemy.
With Him there is no fear.

Purity

*So you also must consider yourselves dead
to sin and alive to God in Christ Jesus.
Let not sin therefore reign in your mortal
body, to make you obey its passions.*

(Romans 6:11–12)

IN 2018, I MADE a trip to the mall for a gift card and visited the Christian bookstore. While chatting with the manager, she informed me that Eboni Johnson would be the first person to have a book signing there at the store.

"What is the name of the book she wrote?" I asked.

"*Half Flesh Half Spirit: The Life of an Ex-Fornicator*," the manager said, then added, "Once I started reading it, I couldn't put it down."

At that time, I mentioned that my book would hopefully be ready for publication at some point in the future.

"You can speak to Eboni about her book signing. She's very nice and could give you beneficial advice." She stepped away and when she came back, she gave me Eboni's telephone number. She said she'd checked with Eboni by phone to make sure it was OK.

We set up an appointment and sat across from each other at the food court in the mall just prior to her book signing. She's a very pretty African American woman in her thirties with black braided hair and brown eyes.

Something about the title of her book struck a chord in me. How could I not ask about it? It is not a popular topic but it is an important one as a member of the Christian community.

"It was very embarrassing to write this kind of book but I felt led by God to do so, and it became therapeutic for me."

Eboni was open and voluble that day, ruminative. Stories from childhood and adulthood came tumbling out on top of one another as she launched into her next heart-wrenching experiences.

"How did this big change come about?" I asked. "What turned you around, Eboni?"

"I was familiar with the Word of God but I didn't have a relationship with God," she said. "Lust had me blind."

"How did the change take place?"

"I went back to church and Prophetess, my mentor at the time, did not sugarcoat anything. She gave me the truth, whether I wanted to hear it or not. But I didn't take heed to the warnings—the dreams God was giving me, and I went back to it." She confessed that the patterns and habits that at first seemed like fun, had eventually led to severe depression and abuse. Then she said she came to the end of herself. "I surrendered and repented and asked God to help make me holy and to help me follow His instructions concerning me getting out of that sexual relationship and the strongholds that kept me in bondage."

"How were your prayers answered, Eboni?"

She reflected for a moment before responding. "I heard Romans 6:11–12 and went over and over it in my mind. I had to respond to temptation as a dead woman would, to reckon myself to be dead to sin and alive to Christ."

If we are in Christ, we are new creations. The former has passed away. The new has come (2 Corinthians 5:17). The gospel can change us through the power of the Spirit. But you must be willing to put in the effort to come out of your old lifestyle and be unwilling to compromise (Ephesians 6:13).

You may be involved with a male friend, and while you say you're just friends, you know it has become more than friendship. Examine your heart. Can you really say that there is justification for a relationship that is not appropriate? Giving in is not an option. This will only bring Satan into the equation, and he'll lead you into bondage.

This transgression has become widespread in the church because it is so easy to justify. The dreadful price of not battling Satan's grasp is costly. Your spiritual freedom is worth fighting for. Stop before it gets worse.

My dad didn't allow me to date in high school. Later, when I gave a young man I liked my address, he knocked on our door soon after, and I saw him from my bedroom window. In no time flat, he was lying on the front lawn, courtesy of my father. Of course, it was upsetting, but later, I felt blessed to have had parents who ingrained values in me. The easiest way to summarize the Bible's teaching on sexuality is to begin with God's blessing of sex only within marriage (Hebrews 13:4, 1 Corinthians 6:19–20). Satan doesn't tell you the consequences of disobeying this biblical principle. If you give in, you will experience depression and heartache, and you'll feel used.

In order to remain sexually pure, here are four things to help you in Eboni's words.

1. **You have to have a prayer life.** You have to cry out to God for help. You don't have just sexual ties. You have soul ties. A soul tie is

like a linkage in the soul realm between two people. It links their souls, which can bring forth both beneficial and negative results. Sometimes, the only way to remove this is through fasting and prayer. I believed that God would deliver me and He did. God hears a sincere prayer.

2. **Read the Word.** The Word of God is cleansing to our soul. The Word also helps in transforming the mind. Just don't read it. Meditate on it. Allow the Word of God to sink in. When you are doing this, it is building up your spirit man so it can stand when temptation presents itself.

3. **Obedience.** I had to be obedient to God's instructions for my life. Did I want to have sex again? Yes! But God would tell me that I didn't need to talk to him [the man] or call him or go over there. And He told me not to watch this on TV. You will never be free if you are not obedient. You have to allow God to lead and guide you. Obedience is better than sacrifice.

4. **Let others help you.** I thank God for my pastor. She would allow me to sleep on her couch when temptation was too strong. God never designs for us to do this thing alone. He gave us the body of Christ so we could have a support system. You need people

who will give you godly counsel—people you can lean on for that support, and who understand what you are going through. Make sure you have someone around you who will hold you accountable.

Sexual purity is one of those things that you have to make up your mind about. No one can do it for you. When you make up your mind, transformation follows. We are transformed by the renewing of the mind. Pull down the strongholds and vain imaginations. It starts with a vision or thought, then becomes an action. Sex is progressive, meaning one act leads to another. It doesn't just happen.

You have to set boundaries and stick to them. Keep your mind on spiritual things. Spend time praying, reading the Word, hanging out with the right people. Then you get through one day, then a week, month, then years. It is a process. Sexual purity allows you to be free to do the will of God without compromise.

Eboni has been celibate, or sexually pure, for eight years. And every day, she has to continue to follow these instructions to remain free. Now, she's living for Jesus. She became an ordained pastor at Alpha & Omega Apostolic Ministries in Palmetto Florida, on June 8, 2019.

A Consecrated Life

A war is waged for our bodies,
A battle against our souls.
We take the stand for righteousness
To be set free from Satan's woes.

God has given us bodily structure,
The truth embedded in God's design
For men and women according to His Word
That must be kept in mind.

Thus, we're not engaged in sexual perversion
That only leads to lust and adultery.
We keep our bodily behavior pure
With surrender of our hearts to Thee.

We claim the victory God won over sin
When He died on the cross.
As a Christian, we entered His death
Now we're free in Christ, not lost.

Never forget the Master is ever with you
He can be your dearest friend
His gracious Spirit resides in you
Your closest confidant to the end.

Hospitality

Beloved, let us love one another, for love is from God, and whoever loves has been born of God and knows God.

(1 John 4:7)

IN THE EARLY 2000s, I was introduced to Lydia Chorpening at a writers conference through a mutual friend. Through the years, our friendship grew through phone calls and letter writing (she lived in Kalona, Iowa). Lydia wrote many books. She was also a freelance writer, an effective speaker, a licensed minister, as well as working with developmentally disabled adults. I admired Lydia's dedication and sincerity to help people get their life back on track. She passed away from cancer in 2017 and is deeply missed, but her words and passion for loving others live on.

Lydia shared many stories with me from her life, and she used to talk to me about hospitality. The dictionary defines "hospitality" as the friendly and generous reception of entertainment of guests, visitors, and strangers. But it seems like a lost art today. We make all sorts of excuses for not receiving Christians who are passing through, including having homes or apartments that are too small. Perhaps it's the added work and inconvenience that keep us from doing so. We forget that when we help or entertain God's people, it is the same as if we were doing it to the Lord Himself (Hebrews 13:2).

Lydia changed her community by being committed to it. Here's how.

"It was 2013," she told me one day, "that the winter weather blasted the northwest area of Wisconsin without warning. And the small town in which I resided at the time was covered with record-breaking amounts of snow by Thanksgiving.

"Frigid winds from the lake slammed our tiny community with crippling effects. As I scooped the snow off our deck and uncovered the gigantic snow-frosted cake in front of the deck, I found it to be our Toyota.

"I looked up and down my street. My next-door neighbor was a Vietnam vet and he was hurting. Others in the area were alone, hurting, and just trying to make ends meet.

"The beginning of winter was worse than usual, and it seemed we were more isolated than ever, so I figured we needed the warmth of each other's friendship. It's the way of seeing the world with kingdom eyes. So I started inviting folks to our 1972 mobile home for soup.

"Soup brought back memories of my grandmother's cooking. Entering her home after school, I could smell the delectable aroma of the apples and cinnamon in her butternut squash soup, simmering on the stove. I loved helping her prepare her savory recipes. It served as the perfect apprenticeship for my life."

I was enthused to hear more of Lydia's plan. "Did you always prepare soup when you invited people over at the mobile home park?"

"Not quite," she said. "I planned a chili dinner for our first round, knowing that chili might be the best bet for everyone. Although we did have chili a couple of times, we seldom had the same soup twice. Potatoes, onions, broccoli, carrots, celery, beans, and corn were a few of the vegetables that found their way into the soup pot. Sometimes I mixed it with ham, chicken, turkey, or beef. But it was always nourishing.

"For the first gathering, I made nice invitations, bundled up in my warmest clothing, and headed out into the blizzard. I knocked on doors, and when I got answers, I left the invitations."

"What was the result?" I asked.

"Tony, a single man who spent a lot of time in bed because of depression, was one of the first to respond. Jeannette, a single mom, brought her six-year-old son. Don, the caregiver of the mobile home park, wobbled in on his cane. Stan and his wife, Sandy—an older couple—hardly ever missed the event. Their son, who is a gourmet cook, was there and brought a big pot of his delicious soup at various times."

Hearing Lydia speak, I thought that food, and our memory of it, goes beyond a recipe. Food offers a powerful, surprising, and uplifting path through difficult events, causing us to feel happy, protected, and cared for—everything we should feel.

"The list went on and on," Lydia continued. "We continued meeting from 5:00-7:00 p.m. each Thursday. The sweetness of friendship started to transform the community. As spring arrived, I hated to announce that soup weather was over, and we'd have to do something else. Everyone had different ideas.

"It went beyond potluck," she said. "Because these events were God-birthed, we had times of prayer and also, times of separate Bible studies. God touched people's hearts. Our little community was experiencing positive changes, and then it happened."

"What happened, Lydia?"

"I faced the test of leaving the community and moving back to our roots in Iowa," she said. "We were packed up and gone in six weeks."

"Have you heard anything since?"

"The community pitched in and continued the neighborhood meal twice a month. I got word that the whole area has been changed."

Lydia sometimes crashed their get-togethers with a phone call and let them know that God loves them and hasn't forgotten them. Her selfless love put the welfare of others before her personal interest.

After hearing Lydia's story, nurturing others became my aim—the deeper meaning of life as Lydia mentioned. Mother Teresa wrote a book titled *A Call to Mercy: Hearts to Love, Hands to Serve.* All of us need such hearts and hands (Luke 14:12–14), now more than ever.

We can all practice hospitality. It provides strategic opportunities to deepen friendships and share the gospel. There's something about opening our homes that results in open hearts. Many churches are trying to use this very method via small groups and are having such great success, but you don't necessarily need a church-sponsored small group.

While writing this chapter, Hurricane Irma made landfall in Florida as a Category 5 storm. My husband and I left town, and when we returned, we were blessed to find that our home and neighbors' homes were spared from the worst effects of the storm. But that does not overshadow the deaths and damage this hurricane season left behind in Florida, Texas, Puerto Rico, and the Caribbean region. I couldn't help but wonder what I would do for others if I lived in the hardest-hit areas. I would have certainly wanted to minister to the hurting in some tangible way.

In the past few months, who has crossed your mind as someone you can help? Perhaps it's an acquaintance who is suffering from cancer in the hospital. Or maybe you can invite your neighbor who lives alone or is divorced and needs strengthening. Even a greeting card or phone call can mean so much to someone who might need encouragement or cheer to let him or her know you care. God has created us to do good works (Ephesians 2:10). In 3 John, John encourages us to take care of the brethren. How can you do so, starting today?

Fruitful Valley

Through the valley where Christ assigns us

There His eyes will precisely guide us

As we focus on our Lord Christ Jesus

He'll turn our faith into firm trust.

We're given seed that God had programmed
To be faithful in our lowest place;
In faith, this seed must first be planted
It will be fruitful by His majestic grace.

In this valley, we've been appointed
To lift our voices with joyful sound,
To make praise echo amid the trials
Where only tests make grace abound.

We'll bear a harvest in our valley.
Fertilizing our place with abounding song.
We break forth into singing amid the mountains,
Finding grace and love were there all along.

As we pass through our tests and our valleys
And share with our neighbors nearby
We gain strength to climb the next mountain
What crops of faith and peace we find.

Praying for
Your Children

*And these words that I command you today
shall be on your heart. You shall teach them
diligently to your children, and shall talk of
them when you sit in your house, and when
you walk by the way, and when you lie down,
and when you rise.*

(Deuteronomy 6:6–7)

ST. AUGUSTINE WASN'T ALWAYS the man we've
come to admire. An August 27, 2018 article on *The
Federalist* website titled "Saint Augustine's Mother
Monica Richly Illustrates the Power of Mothers
and of Prayer" by Casey Chalk says he wandered
in sin during his youth with no seeming regard for
the faith of his mother Monica. She is said to have
prayed, fasted, and wept over Augustine's lifestyle.

Eventually, he left Rome, but his mother followed him, continuing to storm the gates of heaven for his soul. She prayed for him for seventeen years before he was finally converted to Christ.

This is the ministry to which mothers are called. When I was a young mother, part of me thought I could save my sons from suffering, which of course, was absurd (John 15:5). They had to go through their struggles.

Proverbs 31:2 says, "What are you doing, my son? What are you doing, son of my womb? What are you doing, son of my vows?" The reference to "son of my vows" discloses a mother's concerns for her child's benefit. What a great duty we have as mothers to pray every day for our children in a gospel-centered approach. The questions in this verse illuminated and inspired me to pray as a hedge of protection for my children, so God could direct their steps and give them the spirit of discernment against Satan's tactics (Colossians 1:9–12). Cooperation with God in prayer opens the door to His grace and casts out the temptations of the enemy.

The Scriptures inform us how to pray, and we can certainly apply all the admonitions we find in the Bible to prayers for our children. Mark 11:24 tells us to pray in faith. 1 John 5:14 says to pray in conformity with the will of God. Luke 18:1–8 says to pray with persistence. And Psalm 66:18

tells us to make sure we don't have any unconfessed sin in our own life.

God desperately wants to help your children. Hold His promise from Isaiah 49:15–16 in your heart so your children are not forgetful of Him: "Can a woman forget her nursing child, that she should have no compassion on the son of her womb? Even these may forget, yet I will not forget you. Behold, I have engraved you on the palms of my hands; your walls are continually before me."

It was a warm April afternoon in 2017 when I met Lacinda Damsgard via phone. She's the daughter of my friend Lydia Chorpening. Lacinda had called to let me know that she heard a message I had left on her mother's phone while visiting her when her mom was ill. Then she said something that took my breath away.

"I have sad news," Lacinda said. "My mom passed away."

After the initial shock, my memory raced back to the great example Lydia set. She was lionhearted in her faith, and she had great belief in the power of prayer for her children. I reflected back to Lydia's involvement in children's ministry in her church and how she was determined to broaden it with prayer. In 2015, she wrote and illustrated her book *The Tale of Sum Bunny*—a coloring book for young children, ages four to seven. It offered parents the opportunity to guide their children in the Lord with devotional concepts, arresting insights, reflections, and Scripture on every page.

After Lacinda and I talked on the phone that day, we began to communicate by letter. She lived in Minnesota while I lived in Florida. It wasn't long before I discovered that Lacinda had four children—three daughters and a son, ranging from fourteen years down to seven. I heard more and more about Lacinda's children, their activities, comings and goings, and their liveliness and zeal. I couldn't help but wonder what Lacinda's prayer life was like for her children. Was she following her mother's example?

I thought about the role that Lois, Timothy's Jewish grandmother, played in equipping Timothy for his life, which I'd read about in Scripture (2 Timothy 1:5). And then through her daughter, Eunice, who picked up where Lois left off in teaching Timothy the great truths of faith and prayer. What an excellent spiritual heritage Timothy had.

At the beginning of this year, I finally had the opportunity to ask Lacinda some questions. The following is our conversation.

"What was your early upbringing like?" I asked.

"The home I grew up in was a place of prayer, worship, and faith. Any day of the week, I could wake up to my parents' voices singing praises and bringing requests before their heavenly Father.

"My mom instituted family prayer at bedtime and passed on a knowledge of the importance of prayer to her children, which was the top of her priorities. I learned that prayer is an essential part of the Christian's life."

"What was that like?"

"We would be spread around my parents' bed as we knelt. Mom, Dad, myself, and my two sisters. My siblings and I buried our faces into an heirloom quilt. And each of us waited for our turn to pray aloud. We gave thanks for multitudes of grace and blessings, then lifted numerous more cares and concerns to the Lord. In addition, Saturday was a designated family prayer time.

"We had a constant awareness of being in the presence of Jesus and truly believing that God welcomed our cares on Him, as well as finding rest in communion with Him. Our whole family often committed portions of Scripture to memory—ten to fifteen verses at a time. From these stories of Scripture, she laid the foundation for so many of our prayers, finding God's promises and attributes to vocalize and build our faith.

"Many times in my parenting, I have been so thankful for my mother's example of prayer and trusting in the Lord. I also greatly respect the way my mom would pray Scripture. Through her, I grew to love and appreciate what a faith-building experience it can be. Praying for my own children is something that I have grown in over my fourteen years of being a mom. Using Scripture models for prayers has been very helpful during times when my mind wants to wander or I'm simply having trouble addressing the concerns in my heart.

"My greatest desire for my children is that they will love God more than anything else and will trust in Jesus as their Savior. As I pray for assurance of their salvation and for their sanctification, I also pray that they will love, study, and memorize God's Word, grow into a vibrant relationship with God, and be led by and filled with the Holy Spirit. I pray for their hearts and minds to be calibrated to God's Word as they make more decisions on their own. I pray that they will withstand the attacks of Satan and be protected with the armor of God as outlined in Ephesians 6:10–18. I pray for them to develop godly character and to be clothed with humility, wisdom, and courage for the purpose of using their gifts and callings for God's glory and the strengthening of the body of Christ.

"As my children are growing, I have talked about how we can trust God with every detail of our lives. God does not promise His children the absence of difficulties, but He does promise He will work all things for the good of those who love Him, as Romans 8:28 says.

"They are responsible for making wise decisions and choosing thoughts, words, and actions that honor God, but they need God to help them to do these things. When my children are feeling discouraged, depressed, or defiant, we often stop, acknowledge the sin, and then ask God to change their hearts and help them choose strength, joy, and obedience to Him.

"I try to communicate that there is nothing too trivial to pray about. I am thankful for my mother's example of faith in praying without ceasing, casting all anxieties on the Lord, and submitting to His will during both times of joy and times of trial. Prayer is a means that God uses to fulfill His perfect will. Sometimes, God's plan is not what we hoped for, and yet, there is peace knowing that He works what He knows is best. But prayerful dependence must be the consistent attitude of our hearts."

Our conversation left no doubt in my mind that Lydia's prayer legacy had indeed been passed down to the next generation. And it thrilled me to hear Lacinda speak with such great depth and with such a devoted heart. She, like her mother, knew how important it was to pray for her children.

Our children are part of a great spiritual battle—a battle for their souls. We will not win the battle through better parenting techniques or any other way. God must work in the hearts of our children, and He usually does so after we've hit our knees in prayer for them. If I could offer five pieces of advice about praying for your children, I would say this:

1. Pray for your children's particular circumstances, but more importantly, pray that God would shape them into His image (Romans 8:29).
2. Believe that God will answer prayer and receive it (Mark 11:23–24). Ask and it will be given to you (Matthew 7:7, Luke 11:9–10).
3. Do not doubt (James 1:6).
4. Expect great things to result from prayer (James 5:16).
5. After you've prayed, rest in the fact that God works all things according to the counsel of His will (Ephesians 1:11).

When I was praying for my sons when they were growing up, I made specific requests to the Lord. Prayers such as:

- "Lord, let them be aware of their need for you today."
- "Cause them to think of eternity today."
- "Keep them on the narrow path today, Lord."

- "Lead, guide, and protect them as they go to school and spend time with their friends."
- "Give them clear minds and pure hearts as they step out into the world."

Your prayers may be similar. Whatever the case, be as specific as possible as you boldly approach the throne of grace regarding your children.

High Hope in Prayer

Have hope! Let not your heart be troubled

God is near to all hearts who pray.

His compassions are new every morning;

There's rest in His love in this day

His unfailing love surrounds you

With brightness of His presence and care.

His arms encircle and draw you

Dispensing comfort in place of despair.

Have hope! His Word assures that He is loyal

In repentance comes mercy each day.

He never forsakes those who seek Him

And patiently waits in His way.

He's there to uphold and strengthen
As He guides you with His loving hand.
Trust will turn all your grief away,
As time in His presence you spend

Simplicity

*Make me to know your ways, O LORD; teach
me your paths. Lead me in your truth and
teach me, for you are the God of my salvation;
for you I wait all the day long.*

(Psalm 25:4–5)

SEVEN YEARS AGO, AFTER Sunday Mass, I was
leafing through some brochures I picked up at church
and one of them caught my eye. I noticed the words,
"In the footsteps of St. Francis." I turned the brochure
over and noticed a woman's name and long-distance
telephone number. Then I forgot about it.

Later, while participating in our church ministry to the sick, I encountered a woman at the hospital who invited me to her church that offered
classes about living simply, based on the teachings
of St. Francis, prompting my memory of the brochure at church.

When I returned home, I felt impelled to retrieve the brochure from my purse and call that long-distance number. I introduced myself, saying I happened across their information and wanted to know more about their fraternity. I learned that the woman who answered, Misty, had distributed the brochures while visiting the area. As we chatted, our conversation turned personal in a hurry. She shared that she'd recently had an accident using a saw which necessitated stitches in her right hand.

"Do you have someone to help you?" I asked.

"I have one sister and hardly ever see her—she sees me only on my birthday."

Hearing how alone she felt made me sad. She went on to tell me that she was abused and molested when she was younger and that her life was suddenly upended by divorce, leaving her with essentially nothing—not even a house.

"I was in a nightmare of pain, regret, anger, and doubt," she said.

I grew quiet. I should have said more to make her feel less alone, but I wasn't sure what to say.

Her voice hushed to almost a whisper.

"I can't hear you, Misty."

"Oh, I'm sorry. I'm sitting on my couch with my cat, Jud. He has cancer and when he moans, I pet him with my other hand."

Accidently, I let go of the receiver without thought. The sadness in her voice caused something to crack inside me. "Misty, I'll call you back another time."

"I would like to go on," she said to my surprise. "When my mother died two years ago, I couldn't get out of bed. We were so close. I knew I had to dig through the junk inside me so I'd be free from holding judgment and not obsessed with the past, but my inflated ego would not let go."

I assessed the situation and determined that she'd been holding onto judgment against her husband, as well as others who had offended her, only realizing that after her mother died.

"I don't know why we don't see our limitations in the present moment, but we often don't," I said. "The truth should unsettle us, but we justify and defend ourselves at all costs. I can assure myself that my integrity outshines another, yet, in my honest moments, I recognize that I have the same human frailties and flaws."

"I didn't know where to go or who to see. I was searching and then heard about the Portiuncula Fraternity from my church and joined. By doing so, my problem became an opportunity."

"Did it bring the outcome you hoped for?" I asked.

"Oh yes."

She went on to tell me that when we are aware of how our soul works, we can nourish it. Without nourishing our soul, our body holds us back with insistent demands for gratification and prevents us from true transcendence. I found that sentiment to be profound.

"It's been over two years since I joined this order and I couldn't be happier," she said. "We live by the prayer of St. Francis who lived in simplicity and in wonderful harmony with God, others, and himself."

After chatting with Misty, I looked up the prayer. Here's what it says:

Lord, make me an instrument of Thy peace;
where there is hatred let me sow love;
where there is injury, pardon;
where there is doubt, faith;
where there is despair, hope;
where there is darkness, light;
and where there is sadness, joy.

O Divine Master,
grant that I may not so much seek to be
consoled, as to console;
to be understood, as to understand;
to be loved, as to love;
for it is in giving that we receive,
it is in pardoning that we are pardoned,
and it is in dying that we are born to eternal life.[1]

After reading it and spending some time in contemplation, I realized I needed to exercise the same internal simplicity from every distraction in my life if I was going to be responsible to God (James 1:2, Philippians 3:13, 1 Timothy 4:7–9) and truly free to minister to others. After reading the prayer of St. Francis and meditating on it, I had the sense that I was too attached to temporal things—my possessions.

I decided to try a little experiment. I went through our house and removed one to ten items from each room. It was surprising to see how putting forth such a small effort could make such a big difference. So many things had served so little purpose or had lost importance in our home.

My closet was next in line. I began to donate all the whimsical and colorful, including printed blouses and jackets and a variety of dresses and skirts that no longer suited me but that someone else would love.

Once I finished, I headed for our library. Grace-filled Christian books were my absolute downfall. I find that next to the Bible, books are the purest, most complete, most effective means for delivering knowledge and emotion. Initially, I could not part with any of them. Then I jotted down a quote from A. W. Tozer and it became my guide: "The best book is not the one that informs merely, but the one that stirs the reader up to inform himself."[2] I kept only the Christian books that were right for me and released the remainder to friends and family.

Moreover, I found a variety of other types of books to relinquish: health, piano, herb and vitamin, children's, cooking, psychology, and medical. Elias and I filled a multitude of boxes and delivered them to Goodwill and our local library.

The act of clearing stuff uncluttered my mind and I felt lighter. I enjoyed a rejuvenated focus, as we are told to seek first the kingdom of God and His righteousness (Matthew 6:33, Luke 9:24).

Jesus didn't condemn people for owning and enjoying things. God made things and called them very good (Genesis 1:31, Matthew 6:32, 1 Timothy 6:17). He wants us to enjoy them. But Jesus did remind us to put God's kingdom first, and then He will provide what we need.

As a young Christian woman, you are busy with cooking, cleaning, laundry, grocery shopping, and the children. Maybe you even have a job outside of the home. Since your husband is working, too, the two of you might not even see each other all that often. Your family has bills to pay, including a mortgage or rent that takes your breath away every time you think about it.

What if you decided to carve out some time to pray with your husband about the possibility of living with less? Wait until the kids are in bed and the dishes are washed and put away one evening, then talk about what it would look like to live differently than the world. Maybe you could downsize your possessions and move into a smaller house, thereby lowering your mortgage payment. Maybe you could downsize to one car or give up an expensive hobby.

When my husband and I were first married, he had to begin his residency program at the hospital all over again since he wasn't from the United States. He spent all his extra time at home studying for the Educational Commission for Foreign Medical Graduates (ECFMG) certification so he could obtain his medical degree in the U.S. At that time, I worked to help with finances. With sacrifice, our family of four was able to take out a mortgage for a condominium. We also shared one car, and we drove that cozy light blue pinto for many years. I said all of that because I understand that downsizing and living with less is difficult. But it can be done. My husband and I were married for forty-six years, so I still have too much stuff and continue to eliminate things. It's an ongoing process but I've learned that I always feel a little lighter after I rid myself of another round of things.

Seeds of Light

Seize God's glories as they pass
His fullness of truth divine.
How near to cheer our lonely way
In thy mist of shriveled mind.

His Spirit teaches to succumb thy will,
A bona fide of letting go
Of impulsive and enticing desires
Into a barren of faith that flows.

No longer children of this age
With inflammation of one's self,
Nor retaining of lofty expectations
But relying on God as thy help.

Co-laborers with Christ we become
In agreement of what thy heard
To determine all outcome of events
His ways are always right and good.

[1] While attributed to St. Francis, this prayer appears to be written and first published by Father Esther Bouquerel in the December 1912 issue of *La Clochette*.
[2] A.W. Tozer, *Man, the Dwelling Place of God* (Chicago: Moody Publishers, 2018).

Finding Joy
in Surrender

"Abide in me, and I in you. As the branch cannot bear fruit by itself, unless it abides in the vine, neither can you, unless you abide in me."

(John 15:4)

A COUPLE OF YEARS ago, I was referred to my new hairstylist, Kori Hostetler. In addition to her being highly recommended, her salon was close to my house. Immediately after meeting her, I was taken aback by her joyfulness and sweetness. In our conversation, I discovered she was doing volunteer work at her church, teaching art to young boys in the third and fourth grade. I loved viewing the video on her cell phone with these boys who were wiggling, jumping, and dancing to the music Kori set up for them when they entered the room. Even more, I loved hearing about the ways she engaged their senses to not only art but to life as well.

One day, we went out for breakfast and she kept coughing.

"Are you OK, Kori?"

"I'll be all right. We've been living in an apartment and discovered black mold. It was affecting my husband Jesse's health as well as mine, so we had to move. But it was a reminder of so many things to me—how sometimes we can't see something, like sin or the enemy, but if we aren't being careful, it can creep in and make us spiritually sick. Also, I learned how God will always lead us out of something when we are seeking after Him. We were sustained by not giving up. Whether it is prayer, singing, dancing, my art, worship music, loving others, or just crying out in the middle of the mold, He was always present. I can look back and see how He carried us through."

Kori expressed how important the truth of John 15:4 was in her quiet time: "Abide in me, and I in you. As the branch cannot bear fruit by itself, unless it abides in the vine, neither can you, unless you abide in me."

"He used this opportunity to restore me and show me how to have faith and confidence in Him. Jeremiah 31:3–4 tells us that He loved us with an everlasting love, therefore with loving-kindness, He has drawn us to Himself. And it says He will rebuild us. It's such an amazing promise to rest on. Even though our process of transformation doesn't happen overnight, and some days, it feels like we have taken steps backward, He is in the process of giving us a new and clean heart every day."

I recalled that Kori had mentioned that she and her husband visited Ashville, North Carolina, and wanted to move there in the future. And I knew they had been praying about it, so I asked her about how her life was going in their apartment, wondering if she would talk about a possible impending move.

"Well, reluctantly, I wanted to decorate it. I purchased a new dining room table and some other things, but it felt like a kiss of death. It made me feel rooted in a city I no longer wanted to live in. I couldn't help but wonder how feeling settled and finding community was going to get me to North Carolina. Creating a home felt like I was telling God, 'Oh, hey, I'm happy here. Please don't change my life.' I didn't want to be stuck in that apartment forever. My whole goal was to figure out a way to get to North Carolina, but that was my problem. I was trying to figure it out, rather than submitting to God. I felt trapped and filled with anxiety. Moving seemed like the only thing that would make it better."

Kori and her husband did end up moving to North Carolina shortly thereafter, which prompted me to ask her about the moving process and how she stayed focused on God to the point that He released them to move.

"I had consistent quiet time with God, used my giftings to seek after the Lord, and just had open communication with Him. He began to grow my faith and trust in Him, and I got to the point in which the goal of finding God's will for my life had more value and weight than me wanting to relocate to North Carolina. He didn't want control over my life, or yours, in an aggressive way, but rather in a way that showed me that He loved me and only wanted my heart to be at peace. He wanted me to be confident in what He is doing in us at that particular time.

"So I set up the dining room table and stepped into community with a purpose and really began to turn our house into a home. I also kept a journal, and the only thing I would write in it was the date and Bible verses. Many times, God would lead me to look back at my journal and He would use the Scriptures to talk to me and build my confidence more and more in Him. The exposure to His Word brought me such joy.

"I felt like He took a situation in which I felt so much uncertainty and then used it to gain control over my life and trust in Him. It was no longer about me feeling overwhelmed and wanting to run away to a new place. Instead, God settled my soul, then called my husband and me to North Carolina. He showed me how He can take a broken situation and turn it into joy. It reminded me of what Psalm 16:11 says: 'You make known to me the path of life; in your presence there is fullness of joy; at your right hand are pleasures forevermore.' And it reminded me of what Jesus said in John 15:11: 'These things I have spoken to you, that my joy may be in you, and that your joy may be full.'

"God knew my heart, and I felt a huge shift once I finally got to that place of surrender in my relationship with Him. That's when the Holy Spirit started to cultivate other plans in our lives. God was using the things I was reluctant about to help launch us into the path to which He had called us. I got to the point in my quiet time in which I flat out asked the Holy Spirit if He was really calling us to move. I heard a very big and very clear yes.

"During this time, God was telling me, 'This is what I do. I go through everything in your life and get rid of the things that no longer bring you life and weigh you down. I replace it all with joy.' I know the Lord was with us and our decision to move. My faith and confidence in Him had grown that much. The only thing we could do was rest and thrive in

Ashville, North Carolina. My husband is currently supporting us by driving for Uber, and we know God will build us a new business and community in His timing.

"When we are seeking with an open heart to please the Lord, He will turn the things that we used to dread, like doing the dishes, laundry, vacuuming, washing the floors, sweeping, or living in a place we'd rather not live, and He'll transform our old desires into new ones. Finding joy in everyday life is just a switch of perspective. We can choose to let the world weigh us down or we can fight to live in the light that God has put in front of us, if we'll just walk in it."

Kori rejoiced knowing God was using everything to strengthen her faith. We need to assess where we are resisting Him and acknowledge that He can rescue us (1 John 1:9, Isaiah 29:13–14), so we will not be drawn away by our desires (James 1:14–15, Galatians 5:24). The next time you feel weighed down in the tasks you have in front of you, relinquish control and allow God to be your navigator. He uses everything for His glory as we surrender to His will.

I've always been passionate about cooking, for reasons beyond my love of food. So much goes into a good meal. First, I prepare food that my family or friends love. Second, I prepare food the way they prefer. And that sets the table, so to speak, for dynamic conversation in which we learn more about one another and have fun. Cooking has always been a love language for me. But I know that God uses even the household chores I don't particularly enjoy. When I engage in them with the right heart attitude, I find that He changes me and fills me with joy.

No task was too menial for Jesus. He was a servant who washed people's feet. How can you or I do any less? When we do so with the right attitude, we will experience His transforming power.

Awaken to Joy

There is joy in work with Jesus,
In His softening glean of love
For aid, for strength, for perseverance
It fits for perfect help above.

Allow the Lord to arrange thy hours
There is value what is done today.
Some very simple, ordinary duty
Can be sacred in a special way.

Fill thy soul in centered prayer,
Know that God will respond to thee.

He knows the end from the beginning
He asks only that we trust to see.

Fill thy soul in reading Scripture
Because of who Jesus says He is,
He longs that we know His goodness
To be filled with uninterrupted bliss.

Fill thy soul with thanksgiving and praise
To thy heavenly Father Almighty
Who carries out His wondrous plan
With founts of gracious love to thee.

Praise and
Thanksgiving

He put a new song in my mouth,
a song of praise to our God. Many will see and
fear, and put their trust in the LORD.

(Psalm 40:3)

IN 2005, I ATTENDED a Christian writers conference in Bradenton, Florida—a dream come true, but ironically, that morning, I woke up feeling intimidated at the thought of meeting with publishers from all over the United States. *How can I show them my shabby manuscript?* I felt so insecure, unskilled, and anxious. I prayed for God's guidance in all details and events. The thought crossed my mind that this was the place God had appointed for me to find inspiration.

Standing in line for lunch, I observed the large crowd and scanned the cafeteria for a seat. In the corner of the room, I noticed a silver-haired lady sitting at the edge of the table with a vacant seat across from her. After placing my lasagna, spinach salad, rice pudding, and coffee on my tray, I darted toward her and introduced myself.

"Hello, I'm Gerry Alderink, from Omaha, Nebraska. I'm so glad you are joining our table." From the moment I met her, it was like talking to an old friend.

A few minutes later, Gerry reached into her leather briefcase, plucked sheets of paper about the attributes of God from her folder, and began passing them to each lady at the table. "Do you want this page or this page?" she said to me.

My eyes studied both sheets of her typed handiwork. I was struck by her obvious love for the Lord. She fruitfully manifested God's majesty and glory.

"I'm not sure which to pick," I said.

"Why not both?"

I accepted her generous offer and thanked her. She didn't hold onto it like it was in short supply; she gave it away freely. I was reminded that we are rivers, not reservoirs. It was the kind of action that brings glory into the most ordinary day. Gerry and I attended different classes during the conference, but we exchanged telephone numbers and kept in touch afterward. As time went on, we built a bridge of friendship.

"I'm going to enroll at the International Center for Biblical Counseling (ICBC) being held in Indianapolis, Indiana," she said one day on the phone.

"How interesting," I said. "Tell me more about it."

"ICBC is a course to equip believers to help people come to a place of freedom from the bondage of the past by sharing about the greatness of God more effectively," she said.

It was a stretch for me emotionally, but I decided to go.

"Let's start with travel arrangements," Gerry said. "Yes, we can even share a room."

We met in Indianapolis. Whims begat surprises. Little did I know the profundity ahead.

Whenever I attended my church, I always encountered God, and I felt close to Him. But after hearing Gerry begin to sing Christian hymns in our hotel room before she'd even unpacked absolutely stunned me. Her foremost thoughts were on the Lord and without a doubt to bring glory to God.

"Why don't you sing with me?" she asked.

With her praise book in hand, I joined her in song right where she was standing, near her bed that was close to the window. She placed the book between us so I could read the words and sing with her. As I did, I felt a loosening inside me. My thoughts slowed and my mind stilled. It was like stumbling upon the holy grail. Worship brought new strength, confidence, awareness of His gracious love, and joy into our private time. Nobody has taught me more about the joy of the Lord than Gerry.

Some of the best moments we had were on our walks at ICBC. Gerry's eyes were opened to everyday epiphanies with a spirit of thanksgiving, and she also demonstrated an impressive resilience. It was of great interest to me to hear about how her God-honoring spirit came about.

"When I was a young girl of two and a half years," she said, "I scratched open measle blisters on my face and streptococcal infection set in—the flesh-eating kind. A significant portion of one side of my face was eaten away and the doctors fought to keep me alive. This was in the days before antibiotics. Through many prayers, God answered, and the infection stopped. I went through nine surgeries between the ages of six to nineteen. My heart's cry to God during those years was, 'Lord, I surrender my life to You and I ask You to make me a blessing to others.'"

Hearing Gerry's story opened my eyes. Rejoicing and giving thanks to God did not come easy for me when things did not go smoothly. My manuscript at the writer's conference was turned down by publishers three years in a row. Rejection hurts, no matter what form it comes in. What I failed to see was that total surrender implies that we lay the entire responsibility on God. We give Him our will for His divine will, so that His will prevails over ours. I had to surrender and say to God, "You can bear the responsibility now." And then I thanked Him with 2 Timothy 2:21 in mind.

Thankfulness, in all aspects—good as well as bad—lifts us above the drudgery of whatever we are facing. Thomas Merton once wrote, "We find true joy when we give up wanting." How true that is. Only then can we have a new song of thankfulness and praise that God puts in our mouth, giving us a new spirit. It reminded me of a fascinating article I'd read about humpbacked whales in *National Geographic* many years ago. The scientists who study the humpbacked whale say their songs are noteworthy because they are continually changing them. New patterns are added and old ones are eliminated so that over a period of time, the whale, in concert with its community, actually sings a whole new song (the whales learn the new songs from other groups of whales when they mingle in feeding grounds). I felt like I was singing a whole new song when I was around Gerry.

The psalmists tell us that the works of God's deliverance in the lives of His people and in creation are many, and they give us reasons to express our praise to Him in new ways. Praise is such a wonderful weapon against our enemy. When we don't seem to be able to get God's attention, we can always turn to praise, worship, and thanksgiving. He lives in these praises that His people bring Him.

In Psalm 40, David gave praise as he recalled God's great deliverances of the past. By doing so, he preserved the memory of what God had done deep in his heart and mind. It became the foundation where he could face his problems of the present and deal with the uncertainties of his future.

This same intersection is where I join in with praise. God took a struggling writer, placed her in writing workshops at a conference, and gave her a song of encouragement. Then God followed up with the profound blessing of allowing me to meet the prominent writer and editor, Lee Warren, who had been invited to teach classes there. He turned out to be a godsend. He ended up editing an article I wrote for *Light and Life* magazine, which was published in May 2006. He also edited my first book. How could I not continue to have a new song in my mouth and a song of praise to our God for all that He is doing and has done? Thanks be to God.

Song of My Soul

What shall I render to the Lord
For all that He has bestowed upon me?

Thou brought me up from the abyss
In answer to my earnest plea.

I praise Thee in this given hour,
Every moment of time as it glides by,
For Thy presence is dwelling in me
With You in me—You hear every cry.

I praise Thee for thy vast mercy,
How great were my sin and my guilt.
What a Savior who died to win me
And the loving friendship it has built.

I praise Thee for thy saving grace
That banishes all my fears
And brings endurance to victory
Through each day and every year.

I praise Thee my precious Jesus
There is no one who loves like Thou
Thy kindness will never fail me
Now humbly at Thy feet I bow.

Teaching the Beatitudes to Children

Blessed is the man who walks not in the counsel of the wicked, nor stands in the way of sinners, nor sits in the seat of scoffers; but his delight is in the law of the LORD, and on his law he meditates day and night.

(Psalm 1:1–2)

THE SERMON ON THE Mount, or the Beatitudes (from the Latin word "blessings"), describes how one receives the blessings of the Lord. In 2011 and 2014, my husband Elias and I felt blessed to journey to the Holy Land where we visited the Church of the Beatitudes on a hill overlooking the Sea of Galilee, Capernaum, and Tabgha. It was there that Jesus preached the greatest ethical teaching ever recorded.

In these Beatitudes, Jesus lays down the greatest laws of holiness. The old Law was in the form of restrictions ("thou shall not"), but Jesus's new teaching was in the form of the blessings one receives when following it. The Beatitudes appear in two different versions in the Gospels (Matthew 5:3–12, Luke 6:20–22).

Standing near the Mount of Beatitudes in Israel, I felt a sense of fulfillment, but at the same time, I knew it was transitory, a fleeting moment. External contentment is based on life's current circumstances. In the Beatitudes, Jesus was referring to being blessed with internal happiness. The Beatitudes include eight true blessings: not only for us but for our children. As children learn and embrace the Beatitudes, they will guide them through life. They commend poverty of spirit, meekness, mercy, purity of heart, kindness, love, harmony, compassion, and peace.

This is not the easiest time to be raising children. Traditional morals and values are being swept away by those who refuse to be governed by, "Thus said the Lord." We, as parents, feel the tension being forced upon our children by today's music, entertainment, and social media. Our culture is telling young people that life is all about them. We even see t-shirts emblazoned with mottos such as, "It's all about me."

The world claims to offer its own version of techniques for success, but those promises can be disappointingly empty. As a parent, we can't protect our children from the pain of this world, but we have been given a fantastic opportunity to set them on the path that God had in mind for them.

If you need a little help to understand the background of the Beatitudes, Psalm 1:1–3 is the place to check. It says the person who flourishes and prospers is the one who meditates on the Law of God. Teaching your children the Beatitudes will give them a good start in life so their faith won't be easily shaken when hardship comes. Deuteronomy 6:6–7 calls believers to teach their children every day. So let's dive into the Beatitudes and see how we can do just that.

- **First Beatitude:** "Blessed are the poor in spirit, for theirs is the kingdom of heaven" (Matthew 5:3).

  Teach your children to embrace humility. The world advises people to make their own way; to pull themselves up by their bootstraps. God wants His followers to depend on Him. He has a plan for their life, but He never expects them to make it on their own apart from Him. Tell them they can never please God without Jesus Christ and that they need to trust in Him with all their hearts (Proverbs 3:5).

- **Second Beatitude:** "Blessed are those who mourn, for they shall be comforted" (Matthew 5:4).

  Teach your children that engaging in sin will never really make them happy. Instead, when they are truly sorry for sinful actions and ask for God's forgiveness, then they will find a special relief and happiness. Teach them to expose their sins, rather than covering them up or pretending they do not exist because Christians are to live in the light. And teach them to express true godly sorrow that leads to repentance so they won't want to continue in their sin (2 Corinthians 7:10).

- **Third Beatitude:** "Blessed are the meek, for they shall inherit the earth" (Matthew 5:5).

  Teach your children true biblical meekness, which is rooted in humility. Matthew Henry wrote this in his commentary about meekness: "The meek are those who quietly submit themselves to God, to his word and to his rod, who follow his directions, and comply with his designs, and are gentle towards all men (Titus 3:2); who can bear provocation without being inflamed by it; are either silent, or return a soft answer; and who can show their displeasure when there is occasion for it." Teach your children that living God's way won't make them the most popular people, but it is the only way to be inwardly happy. Tell them that Jesus is their example and that the Holy Spirit will help them (Philippians 4:13, Romans 8:14).

- **Fourth Beatitude:** "Blessed are those who hunger and thirst for righteousness, for they shall be satisfied" (Matthew 5:6).

    Teach your children that loving and pleasing God is their first priority, and He will give them everything they need (Psalm 37:4). And teach them that nothing in the world will give them satisfaction like reading God's Word and then living to please Him. Holiness brings happiness. As your children hunger and thirst for righteousness, they will not be embarrassed about walking with the Lord (Matthew 6:33).

- **Fifth Beatitude:** "Blessed are the merciful, for they shall receive mercy" (Matthew 5:7).

Since God forgives us and shows mercy to us, we can do the same for others. Teach your children that being kind to others brings special happiness. When someone is hurt or sad or lonely, true Christians take the time to help and show kindness, even when the person does not deserve it. It is never right to ignore someone who is in need when you can help him or her (Ephesians 4:32).

- **Sixth Beatitude:** "Blessed are the pure in heart, for they shall see God" (Matthew 5:8).

  Teach your children that loving God should be the most important thing in their life. Tell them He is the One they should love the most, and their behavior should show it. They will not gain their greatest satisfaction by focusing on outward appearances but by loving God with all their heart (1 Samuel 16:7). Point them toward godly examples in your faith community—people who are earnestly seeking the Lord.

- **Seventh Beatitude:** "Blessed are the peacemakers, for they shall be called sons of God" (Matthew 5:9).

  Teach your children to help people get along. They need to be people who diffuse situations, rather than people who escalate potential problems (Ephesians 4:3, John 14:27). Tell them to share the gospel with their friends, for there is no greater way to make them peacemakers. Finally, teach them to not talk unkindly about others.

- **Eighth Beatitude:** "Blessed are those who are persecuted for righteousness' sake, for theirs is the kingdom of heaven" (Matthew 5:10).

  Teach your children not to react nor retaliate—to release love instead (Matthew 5:43–48), exercising self-control and leaving their disputes with God. We love others because God first loved us, even when we were His enemies. As a result, how can we do anything other than love our enemies, even though they don't deserve it?

I'd recommend that you start teaching the Beatitudes around the dinner table. To get the full benefit of these meals, don't allow phones or tablets, and turn off the TV. The goal is to not just eat but to get a sense of what's going on in your children's lives and to get a gist of their emotional state. For example, if you notice your talkative daughter or son acting in a withdrawn manner, ask them, "You don't seem like yourself. Are you OK? Did something happen at school?" Right then, you can teach them the Beatitudes.

You can also ask your kids to help you cook or with some other chore, such as walking the dog. Or suggest that they join you on an errand to the store and look for opportunities to talk to them in the car about the Beatitudes. If you happen to see an elderly person struggling with his or her groceries, teach your children meekness by offering to help that person. If you see a husband and wife arguing, model peacemaking for your children by trying to get involved in a loving manner.

Deuteronomy 6 tells us not to miss occasions to talk to our children when we rise up in the morning, when we sit with them, when we walk with them, or when we lie down with them. Making these deeply personal face-to-face connections a priority will help your children grow strong in the Lord. What better way than to teach them the Beatitudes? It also acts as a powerful prevention strategy for keeping their minds on our Lord and maker, Jesus Christ.

The Promises of Joy

Thy insight can be enlightened
With guidance in God's holy ways.
Why not come and look with me
As I share it with you this day?

It's only a few steps away
Within a stone's throw from here
In the center of my dwelling
Where I found my Bible lies near.

How divine is His Holy Word
And His ruling so pure and just
With the truth of His promises
In Christ, we can put our trust.

God's Beatitudes transform feelings
For all who are willing to embrace them
By breaking through all denial
With heavenly steps to begin again.

You'll find His words praiseworthy
They help us see our sin,
For it is grace that saves us
And transforms us from within.

Acknowledgments

MANY THANKS TO THOSE who made this book possible:

To my superb editor, Lee Warren, for his keen insight, dedication, and long-standing support.

I'm also grateful for the wonderful, gentle, and hopeful stories shared with me by Bob Armstrong, Gerry Alderink, Mary Ann Dunlap, Eboni Johnson, Kori Hostetler, Lydia Chorpening, and Lacinda Damsgard.

To my heavenly Father God who has kept watch over my life through all these years, even when there was a lack of harkening to Him on my part.

About the Author

DISTRACTIONS AND BUSYNESS WERE keeping
Mary F. Caltenco from seeing God's work around
her. So, on her journey in life, she joined a Bible
study group to begin a closer, more intimate walk
with God. God began placing her with other women
to be a means of enlightenment to His incoming
message, as well as His grace and blessings in her
life. Through these insights, she seeks to gently
offer readers hope and wisdom from God's Word,
in addition to divine quotes she has collected over
the years and poems she has composed.

Mary F. Caltenco is an inspirational author
and a devoted woman of faith. She enjoys reach-
ing out to women in churches and communities
to encourage, comfort, and edify them through
God's love and His Word. She has written for *Light
and Life* magazine, been involved in Bible Study
Fellowship for eight years, and has trained at the
International Center for Biblical Counseling. She
has also visited Israel on a pilgrimage to retrace
the steps of Jesus twice (2011 and 2014).

www.ingramcontent.com/pod-product-compliance
Lightning Source LLC
Chambersburg PA
CBHW022307060426
42446CB00007BA/745